THE LOVE DARE

A 40-Day Challenge to Strengthen Your Relationship

By

Olivia Cole

TABLE OF CONTENTS

Introduction

Love is a beautiful thing, but it's not always easy. Relationships take work and effort to maintain and grow over time. Whether you're in a new relationship or have been married for years, it's important to invest time and energy into strengthening your connection with your partner.

That's where "The Love Dare" comes in. This book is a 40-day challenge designed to help you deepen your love and commitment to your partner. Each day, you'll be presented with a new dare that challenges you to love your partner in a specific way.

These dares are not just suggestions or ideas - they are actionable steps that you can take to show your partner that you care. They range from simple gestures like saying "I love you" to more challenging tasks like practicing forgiveness and letting go of grudges.

But "The Love Dare" is not just about completing tasks or ticking off a to-do list. It's about developing a mindset of love and intentionality in your relationship. By committing to this 40-day challenge, you'll learn to view your partner in a new light and cultivate a deeper, more meaningful connection.

So if you're ready to take your relationship to the next level, join us on this journey. Let's start with Day 1 and see where this love dare takes us.

Part I

Basics of Love

Love is a foundational aspect of any relationship, but what does it really mean to love someone? In this section, we'll explore some of the key elements of love and how they can strengthen your relationship.

Love is Patient

"Love is patient" is one of the most well-known verses about love in the Bible, and for good reason. Patience is a crucial aspect of love, especially in the context of a relationship.

Being patient means taking the time to understand your partner's perspective and needs. It means putting aside your own desires and wants and focusing on what's best for the relationship as a whole. This can be challenging at times, especially when we feel frustrated or overwhelmed by our own emotions.

So how can we practice patience in our relationships? Here are a few ideas:

Practice active listening. When your partner is speaking, give them your full attention. Put down your phone, turn off the TV, and really listen to what they have to say. Ask questions and clarify their meaning if necessary.

Take a deep breath. When you feel yourself getting frustrated or angry, take a moment to pause and breathe deeply. This can help you calm down and approach the situation with more patience and understanding.

Practice empathy. Try to put yourself in your partner's shoes and see the situation from their perspective. This can help you develop more patience and compassion towards them.

Focus on the long-term. Remember that relationships are a marathon, not a sprint. It's important to take the time to build a strong foundation of love and trust, even if that means being patient in the short-term.

By practicing patience in your relationship, you'll build a stronger, more resilient bond with your partner. It takes time and effort, but the rewards are well worth it.

Love is Kind

"Love is kind" is another essential aspect of love. Kindness means treating your partner with warmth, compassion, and understanding. It involves going out of your way to show your partner that you care and appreciate them.

So how can we practice kindness in our relationships? Here are a few ideas:

Show appreciation. Take the time to acknowledge the things your partner does for you and express your gratitude. Say "thank you" and let them know that you appreciate their efforts.

Offer encouragement. Encourage your partner to pursue their dreams and goals, and offer support and reassurance along the way.

Be attentive. Pay attention to your partner's needs and desires, and try to fulfill them whenever possible. This can be as simple as making their favorite meal or planning a surprise date night.

Be compassionate. When your partner is going through a tough time, be there for them with a listening ear and a shoulder to lean on. Show them that you care and are there to support them.

Practice forgiveness. Kindness also involves being willing to forgive your partner when they make mistakes. Remember that we all make mistakes, and showing forgiveness and understanding can go a long way in strengthening your relationship.

By practicing kindness in your relationship, you'll create a positive and supportive atmosphere that will help your love thrive. It takes effort and intentionality, but the rewards are well worth it.

Love is Not Selfish

At its core, love is not about us - it's about our partner. Love requires us to put the needs of our partner before our own and to act with generosity and selflessness. This can be challenging at times, especially when we're used to thinking about ourselves first.

So how can we practice selflessness in our relationships? Here are a few ideas:

Make compromises. Relationships involve give and take. Be willing to compromise and find solutions that work for both you and your partner.

Show generosity. Generosity doesn't have to be big or extravagant - it can be as simple as making your partner's favorite meal or surprising them with a thoughtful gift.

Prioritize your partner's happiness. Ask yourself: "What can I do to make my partner happy today?" By focusing on their happiness and well-being, you'll create a stronger bond of love and trust.

Be willing to apologize. When you make a mistake, be willing to take responsibility and apologize to your partner. This shows that you value their feelings and are committed to the relationship.

Communicate openly. Open and honest communication is key to a healthy relationship. Make sure you're listening to your partner's needs and concerns, and sharing your own thoughts and feelings as well.

By practicing selflessness in your relationship, you'll build a stronger, more compassionate bond with your partner. It takes effort and intentionality, but the rewards are well worth it.

Love is Thoughtful

One of the most important aspects of love is thoughtfulness. Being thoughtful means considering your partner's needs and desires and going out of your way to make them feel loved and appreciated. It involves small gestures and acts of kindness that can make a big difference in your relationship.

So how can we practice thoughtfulness in our relationships? Here are a few ideas:

Pay attention to the little things. Take note of the things your partner likes and dislikes, and try to incorporate those into your daily interactions. For example, if your partner loves a certain type of tea, surprise them with a cup in the morning.

Plan surprises. Surprise your partner with thoughtful gestures and surprises that show you care. This could be anything from leaving a sweet note on their pillow to planning a surprise weekend getaway.

Listen actively. When your partner is speaking, make sure you're actively listening and engaging with what they're saying. Ask questions and show interest in their thoughts and feelings.

Be considerate. Think about how your actions will affect your partner and try to be considerate of their feelings. This could be as simple as taking the time to clean up after yourself or being mindful of how loud you're being.

Show affection. Physical touch is an important aspect of love, so make sure you're showing affection to your partner regularly. This could be as simple as holding hands or giving them a hug when they come home from work.

By practicing thoughtfulness in your relationship, you'll create a stronger bond of love and appreciation with your partner. It takes effort and intentionality, but the rewards are well worth it.

Love is Not Rude

Rudeness can be a major barrier to love and can cause hurt and resentment in our relationships. Love requires us to treat our partner with respect and kindness, even in moments of frustration or disagreement.

So how can we avoid being rude in our relationships? Here are a few ideas:

Watch your tone. The way we say things is just as important as what we say. Make sure you're speaking to your partner in a kind and respectful tone, even when you're feeling upset or frustrated.

Avoid insults and name-calling. Words can be hurtful, so make sure you're not using insults or name-calling in your interactions with your partner. Stick to constructive feedback and productive conversations.

Listen actively. Show your partner that you're listening and engaged in what they're saying. This means putting down your phone, maintaining eye contact, and responding thoughtfully to their comments.

Practice empathy. Try to put yourself in your partner's shoes and understand their perspective. This will help you avoid being dismissive or condescending in your interactions.

Be polite and courteous. Simple gestures like saying "please" and "thank you" can go a long way in creating a culture of kindness and respect in your relationship.

By practicing respect and kindness in your relationship, you'll create a more loving and positive atmosphere that will help your love thrive. It takes effort and intentionality, but the rewards are well worth it.

Love is Forgiving

One of the most important aspects of love is forgiveness. Inevitably, there will be times when we hurt or disappoint our partners, and forgiveness is essential in order to move forward and maintain a healthy relationship.

So how can we practice forgiveness in our relationships? Here are a few ideas:

Acknowledge the hurt. It's important to acknowledge the pain you've caused your partner and take responsibility for your actions. This means apologizing sincerely and making a commitment to do better in the future.

Let go of grudges. Holding onto grudges and resentment will only serve to poison your relationship. Instead, make a conscious effort to let go of anger and bitterness and choose to forgive your partner.

Practice empathy. Try to understand your partner's perspective and why they may have acted the way they did. This will help you find compassion and forgiveness, even in difficult situations.

Communicate openly. Make sure you're communicating openly and honestly with your partner about your feelings and needs. This will help you work together to find solutions and move past any hurt or pain.

Be patient. Forgiveness is a process, and it may take time to fully heal and move forward. Be patient with yourself and your partner and commit to working through any issues together.

By practicing forgiveness in your relationship, you'll create a stronger and more resilient bond with your partner. It takes effort and vulnerability, but the rewards are well worth it.

Part II

The Power of Love

Love has an incredible power to transform and enrich our lives. When we approach our relationships with love and kindness, we create a positive and supportive atmosphere that allows us to grow and thrive together.

Love Makes Good Impressions

First impressions matter, and this is true in our relationships as well. When we show love and kindness to our partner, we make a positive impression that can help build a strong and lasting connection.

Here are a few ways to make good impressions in your relationship:

Show appreciation. Let your partner know that you appreciate them and value their presence in your life. This can be as simple as saying "thank you" or expressing gratitude for something they've done.

Practice good communication. Make sure you're communicating clearly and effectively with your partner. This means listening actively, expressing yourself clearly, and being open to feedback and constructive criticism.

Be present. Show your partner that they have your full attention by being present and engaged in your interactions. This means putting down your phone, maintaining eye contact, and actively participating in conversations.

Be respectful. Treat your partner with respect and kindness, even in moments of frustration or disagreement. Avoid name-calling, insults, and other forms of disrespect.

Show affection. Physical touch and affection can help build intimacy and connection in your relationship. Make sure to show your partner affection in ways that are meaningful to them.

By making good impressions in your relationship, you'll create a positive and supportive atmosphere that will help your love thrive. It takes effort and intentionality, but the rewards are well worth it.

Love Respects

Respect is a crucial element of any healthy relationship. When we show respect to our partner, we demonstrate that we value their thoughts, feelings, and needs. This creates a sense of safety and security in the relationship, allowing us to build a strong and lasting connection.

Here are a few ways to show respect in your relationship:

Listen actively. When your partner is speaking, make sure you're fully engaged and actively listening. This means avoiding distractions, maintaining eye contact, and responding appropriately to what they're saying.

Value their opinions. Your partner's thoughts and opinions matter, and it's important to show that you respect and value them. This means considering their input and incorporating it into your decision-making process.

Avoid criticism and judgment. Criticizing and judging your partner is a form of disrespect. Instead, focus on communicating your own needs and feelings in a respectful and constructive way.

Keep commitments. Keeping your promises and commitments is a way of showing respect to your partner. This means following through on your agreements, even when it's difficult or inconvenient.

Show appreciation. Make sure your partner knows that you appreciate and value them. This can be as simple as saying "thank you" or expressing gratitude for something they've done.

By showing respect in your relationship, you'll create a strong foundation for love and intimacy. It takes effort and intentionality, but the rewards are well worth it.

Love is Responsible

In any relationship, both partners have a responsibility to each other. When we take responsibility for our actions and choices, we create a sense of trust and dependability in the relationship. This allows us to build a strong and lasting connection based on mutual respect and care.

Here are a few ways to be responsible in your relationship:

Own up to your mistakes. When you make a mistake, take responsibility for it and apologize. This shows that you value your partner's feelings and are committed to making things right.

Keep your commitments. Keeping your promises and following through on your commitments is a way of showing respect and care for your partner. This means being reliable and dependable, even when it's difficult or inconvenient.

Communicate honestly. Honesty is a key element of any responsible relationship. Be honest with your partner about your thoughts, feelings, and needs, even when it's uncomfortable or difficult.

Support each other. Show support and encouragement for your partner's goals and dreams. This means being there for them when they need help, and celebrating their successes along the way.

Make decisions together. In any partnership, it's important to make decisions together. This means considering each other's opinions and needs, and finding solutions that work for both of you.

By being responsible in your relationship, you'll create a strong and dependable foundation for love and intimacy. It takes effort and intentionality, but the rewards are well worth it.

Love Communicates

Communication is key to any healthy relationship. When we communicate openly and honestly with our partner, we create a sense of trust and intimacy in the relationship. This allows us to build a strong and lasting connection based on mutual understanding and care.

Here are a few ways to communicate effectively in your relationship:

Listen actively. When your partner is speaking, make sure you're fully engaged and actively listening. This means avoiding distractions, maintaining eye contact, and responding appropriately to what they're saying.

Express yourself clearly. Be clear and direct when expressing your thoughts, feelings, and needs. This helps to avoid misunderstandings and ensures that your partner knows what's important to you.

Avoid blame and criticism. Blaming and criticizing your partner is a surefire way to create conflict and distance in your relationship. Instead, focus on communicating your own needs and feelings in a respectful and constructive way.

Use "I" statements. Using "I" statements (e.g. "I feel hurt when you don't listen to me") instead of "you" statements (e.g. "You never listen to me") can help to avoid defensiveness and encourage productive dialogue.

Show empathy. Put yourself in your partner's shoes and try to understand their perspective. This helps to create a sense of empathy and understanding in the relationship.

By communicating effectively in your relationship, you'll create a strong and intimate connection with your partner. It takes effort and intentionality, but the rewards are well worth it.

Love is Committed

One of the most important aspects of any successful relationship is commitment. When we're committed to our partner, we're willing to put in the effort and make sacrifices to build a strong and lasting connection. This means being there for our partner through the ups and downs of life, and working together to overcome challenges.

Here are a few ways to show commitment in your relationship:

Be loyal. Loyalty is an important aspect of commitment. This means being faithful and true to your partner, and standing by their side no matter what.

Put in the effort. Building a strong relationship takes effort and intentionality. Make sure you're putting in the time and energy to nurture your connection with your partner.

Be willing to make sacrifices. Sometimes, being committed means making sacrifices for the good of the relationship. This might mean compromising on certain issues, or putting your partner's needs ahead of your own.

Work through challenges together. No relationship is without its challenges. When you're committed to your partner, you're willing to work through these challenges together, rather than giving up at the first sign of difficulty.

Make your relationship a priority. Commitment means prioritizing your relationship above other things in your life. This means making time for your partner, even when you're busy or stressed.

By showing commitment in your relationship, you'll create a strong and lasting connection with your partner. It takes effort and intentionality, but the rewards are well worth it.

Love Cherishes

To cherish someone means to hold them dear, to value them, and to show them deep affection and care. When we cherish our partner, we create a strong and lasting bond based on love, respect, and admiration.

Here are a few ways to show that you cherish your partner:

Express gratitude. Make sure your partner knows how much you appreciate them. Express gratitude for the things they do, and for who they are as a person.

Show affection. Small gestures of affection, like holding hands or giving a hug, can go a long way in showing your partner how much you care.

Prioritize their needs. Make your partner's needs and desires a priority in your life. This means taking the time to listen to them, and making sure they feel heard and valued.

Support their dreams. Encourage your partner to pursue their dreams and passions, and be their biggest cheerleader along the way.

Celebrate milestones. Celebrate important milestones in your relationship, like anniversaries and special occasions. This shows your partner that you cherish the time you've spent together, and look forward to the future.

By cherishing your partner, you'll create a strong and lasting connection based on love, respect, and admiration. It takes effort and intentionality, but the rewards are well worth it.

Part III

The Proof of Love

Love is more than just a feeling - it's a choice that we make every day. When we choose to love someone, we commit to putting their needs ahead of our own, and to showing them love and care in both big and small ways.

Love Fights Fair

Disagreements and arguments are a natural part of any relationship. However, how we handle those conflicts can make all the difference in the health and longevity of our relationship. When we fight fair, we communicate effectively and respectfully, and work together to find a solution that works for both parties.

Here are a few ways to fight fair in your relationship:

Stay respectful. No matter how heated the argument gets, it's important to stay respectful towards your partner. Avoid using name-calling or belittling language, and focus on the issue at hand.

Listen actively. Make sure you're really listening to your partner's point of view, and not just waiting for your turn to speak. Reflect back what they're saying to ensure you understand their perspective.

Stay focused on the issue. Don't bring up past grievances or unrelated issues in the midst of an argument. Stay focused on the problem at hand, and work together to find a solution.

Take a break if needed. Sometimes, emotions can run high during an argument. If you or your partner need a break to cool down, take it. Agree to come back to the conversation at a later time.

Work towards a solution. Instead of trying to "win" the argument, focus on finding a solution that works for both parties. This may require compromise and creative problem-solving.

By fighting fair in your relationship, you'll create a strong and healthy connection based on effective communication and mutual respect. It takes effort and intentionality, but the rewards are well worth it.

Love is Accountable

Accountability is an essential component of any healthy relationship. When we hold ourselves and our partners accountable for our actions and decisions, we create a foundation of trust and respect.

Here are a few ways to practice accountability in your relationship:

Take responsibility for your actions. When you make a mistake, own up to it and take responsibility for your actions. This shows your partner that you're willing to be accountable for your behavior.

Set clear boundaries. Establish clear boundaries and expectations for your relationship, and hold yourself and your partner accountable for upholding them.

Check in regularly. Regularly check in with your partner to make sure you're both on the same page, and to address any issues or concerns that arise.

Practice forgiveness. When your partner makes a mistake, practice forgiveness and offer them the opportunity to make amends.

Seek outside support if needed. If you're struggling with accountability in your relationship, consider seeking the help of a therapist or counselor.

By practicing accountability in your relationship, you'll create a strong and healthy connection based on trust and respect. It takes effort and intentionality, but the rewards are well worth it.

Love Values Unity

Unity is a key component of any healthy and thriving relationship. When we value unity, we prioritize the health and wellbeing of our relationship over our individual wants and needs.

Here are a few ways to prioritize unity in your relationship:

Work together towards shared goals. Identify shared goals and work together as a team to achieve them. This will help you feel more connected and united in your partnership.

Communicate openly and honestly. Open and honest communication is key to creating a sense of unity in your relationship. Make sure you're communicating regularly with your partner, and sharing your thoughts, feelings, and concerns with them.

Practice compromise. When you're in a relationship, it's important to practice compromise and be willing to meet your partner halfway. This will help you both feel heard and valued.

Celebrate each other's successes. Celebrate your partner's successes and accomplishments, and be there to support them through their challenges and setbacks. This will help you feel more connected and united in your partnership.

Seek help if needed. If you're struggling to find unity in your relationship, consider seeking the help of a therapist or counselor.

By prioritizing unity in your relationship, you'll create a strong and healthy connection based on mutual respect and a shared sense of purpose. It takes effort and intentionality, but the rewards are well worth it.

Love Speaks Truth

Honesty is a foundational component of any healthy and thriving relationship. When we speak truthfully with our partners, we create a sense of trust and respect that strengthens our connection.

Here are a few ways to practice speaking truthfully in your relationship:

Be honest with yourself. Before you can be honest with your partner, you need to be honest with yourself. Take time to reflect on your thoughts, feelings, and actions, and be willing to confront any areas where you may not be living in alignment with your values.

Communicate openly and honestly. Open and honest communication is key to creating a sense of trust and respect in your relationship. Make sure you're communicating regularly with your partner, and sharing your thoughts, feelings, and concerns with them.

Practice active listening. When your partner speaks to you, make sure you're actively listening and trying to understand their perspective. This will help you communicate more effectively and build a stronger sense of trust and respect in your relationship.

Avoid half-truths or white lies. While it may be tempting to tell a half-truth or white lie to spare your partner's feelings, this can ultimately erode trust in your relationship. Instead, practice speaking truthfully, even if it's difficult or uncomfortable.

Seek help if needed. If you're struggling to speak truthfully in your relationship, consider seeking the help of a therapist or counselor.

By practicing honesty and speaking truthfully in your relationship, you'll create a foundation of trust and respect that will strengthen your connection over time. It takes effort and intentionality, but the rewards are well worth it.

Love Demonstrates Grace

Grace is an essential component of any healthy and thriving relationship. When we show grace to our partners, we extend kindness, forgiveness, and understanding, even in the face of difficult circumstances or disagreements.

Here are a few ways to practice demonstrating grace in your relationship:

Practice forgiveness. When your partner makes a mistake or hurts you, practice forgiveness. This doesn't mean ignoring or condoning harmful behavior, but rather choosing to extend compassion and understanding even in the midst of conflict.

Show empathy. Try to understand your partner's perspective and feelings, even when you disagree with them. This can help you demonstrate grace and extend kindness in difficult situations.

Be patient. Relationships take time and effort, and it's important to be patient with your partner as you work through challenges and disagreements. By showing patience, you can create a sense of safety and security in your relationship.

Offer support. When your partner is struggling, offer them support and encouragement. This can help them feel valued and loved, even in difficult times.

Seek help if needed. If you're struggling to demonstrate grace in your relationship, consider seeking the help of a therapist or counselor.

By practicing grace in your relationship, you'll create a strong and healthy connection based on mutual respect and understanding. It takes effort and intentionality, but the rewards are well worth it.

Love Improves

Love is not static - it's a dynamic force that can help us grow and improve as individuals and as a couple. When we approach our relationship with a growth mindset and a willingness to learn, we can create a strong and healthy connection that supports our personal and collective goals.

Here are a few ways to practice improving your relationship:

Practice self-improvement. When we work on improving ourselves, we can bring more positivity and energy into our relationships. Consider setting personal goals and engaging in activities that help you grow as an individual.

Set shared goals. Setting shared goals can help you and your partner work together towards a common vision for your relationship. Whether it's traveling, starting a family, or pursuing a new hobby, shared goals can create a sense of purpose and direction in your relationship.

Celebrate successes. When you and your partner achieve a shared goal or make progress towards a common vision, take time to celebrate and acknowledge your success. This can help build a sense of shared accomplishment and strengthen your connection.

Learn together. Learning new things together can be a fun and rewarding way to improve your relationship. Consider taking a class or workshop together, or exploring a new hobby that you both enjoy.

Seek help if needed. If you're struggling to improve your relationship, consider seeking the help of a therapist or counselor.

By approaching your relationship with a growth mindset and a willingness to learn, you can create a strong and healthy connection that supports your personal and collective goals. It takes effort and intentionality, but the rewards are well worth it.

Part IV

Conclusion

The Results of Love

When we invest in our relationships and practice love daily, we can experience a range of positive results that improve our lives and the lives of those around us. Here are a few of the many results of love:

Greater happiness: Love can bring us happiness and joy, creating a sense of fulfillment and meaning in our lives.

Improved communication: When we practice love, we also practice effective communication, leading to greater understanding and connection with our partners.

Deeper intimacy: Love fosters intimacy, allowing us to feel closer and more connected with our partners on emotional, physical, and spiritual levels.

Increased trust: Love creates a foundation of trust in our relationships, allowing us to feel secure and confident in our connection with our partners.

Greater resilience: When we practice love and invest in our relationships, we become more resilient in the face of challenges and difficulties.

Improved mental health: Love can improve our mental health, leading to greater emotional stability and wellbeing.

Increased longevity: Studies have shown that strong, loving relationships can lead to increased longevity and improved overall health.

By practicing love daily and investing in our relationships, we can experience these and many other positive results that improve our lives and the lives of those around us. It takes effort and intentionality, but the rewards are well worth it.

Appendix: The Love Dare Daily Challenge Calendar

Week 1:
Day 1: Love is patient
Day 2: Love is kind
Day 3: Love is not selfish
Day 4: Love cherishes
Day 5: Love is thoughtful
Day 6: Love is not rude
Day 7: Love rejoices in truth

Week 2:
Day 8: Love bears all things
Day 9: Love believes all things
Day 10: Love hopes all things
Day 11: Love endures all things
Day 12: Love never fails
Day 13: Love fights fair
Day 14: Love is accountable

Week 3:
Day 15: Love values unity
Day 16: Love respects
Day 17: Love communicates

Day 18: Love is committed
Day 19: Love is responsible
Day 20: Love makes good impressions
Day 21: Love forgives

Week 4:
Day 22: Love demonstrates grace
Day 23: Love is not jealous
Day 24: Love speaks truth
Day 25: Love improves
Day 26: Love is not easily angered
Day 27: Love thinks the best
Day 28: Love is a covenant

Week 5:
Day 29: Love shows honor
Day 30: Love promotes intimacy
Day 31: Love seeks to understand
Day 32: Love brings unity
Day 33: Love is humble
Day 34: Love is content
Day 35: Love is a responsible provider

Week 6:
Day 36: Love protects

Day 37: Love accepts
Day 38: Love models
Day 39: Love inspires
Day 40: Love endures
Reflection: Reflect on your experience and set goals for the future.

Made in the USA
Las Vegas, NV
10 August 2023

75896260R00036